ST SHENOUDA PRESS
8419 Putty Rd,
Putty, NSW, 2330
Sydney, Australia

www.stshenoudapress.com

ISBN 13: 978-0-6455543-7-3

I0202965

SHENOUDA PRESS

Many years ago in a small Egyptian village called Nehisa, close to the Nile River. a little boy was born. His parents were filled with joy because he was their first and only child, they gave him the name Abanoub and loved him dearly. Ever since he was young they taught him to be brave and always follow the Lord Jesus. Abanoub loved Jesus and was excited to learn that Nehisa was special because Jesus and his family visited this place.

Several years after Abanoub was born, his parents passed away. Abanoub knew they were living in Heaven with God. Even though he missed them, Abanoub remembered all their teachings about following Jesus and trusting His promises, so while he missed them very much, he knew that he would see them again in Heaven.

Little Abanoub loved learning about Jesus and going to church. There, he spent time, listening to the priest, understanding the bible and participating in the Holy Sacraments.

One day when Abanoub was twelve years old, he heard the priest encouraging people to be strong, to have hope and have no fear. In those days the Roman Governor was punishing all the Christians. The Governor had a wicked heart, he believed that his statues were gods and he ordered people to worship the statues instead of Jesus, the true God. Many faithful people said no, they were punished and killed by the Governor but their faith in God allowed them to become martyrs in heaven.

When Abanoub heard the story of the martyrs who gave their lives to be with God, he felt that this was a special message for him. Abanoub knew that he had to face the Governor and tell him about his faith and love for Jesus. He wanted people to realise that Jesus our saviour is the true God and that it was wrong to worship statues. He prayed in church that God may strengthen and support him, he had Holy Communion and his heart was filled with peace.

After church Abanoub hurried and gave everything that his parents left him to the poor, he only kept the white tunic he was wearing. He started his journey by walking to the nearby city of Samanoud, remembering the lessons about courage and faithfulness that he was taught since he was a little boy. As he was walking along the green banks of the Nile River, all of a sudden the clouds parted and Archangel Michael appeared in all his glory in front of Abanoub.

Abanoub was filled with excitement as he recognised the Archangel Michael. The Archangel said "Have courage and don't be scared, I am here to prepare you for the challenges you are going to experience in Samanoud over the next three days. God will help you on your mission to show everyone that Jesus is the true God who is the saviour of the world." Archangel Michael blessed Abanoub and his heart was filled with peace and the courage he needed to continue his journey.

Abanoub reached the city of Samanoud and quickly went to meet the local Governor named Lucianus in his palace. He bravely declared his faith in Jesus and refused to worship the statues. Lucianus grew furious as Abanoub refused to follow his orders, he ordered his soldiers to punish Abanoub and throw him in prison. Abanoub was very hurt, Lucianus thought that this would make Abanoub lose faith, but he didn't know that Christian faith grows stronger during difficult times.

Even though Abanoub was hurt, he continued to place all of his trust in God, he remembered a verse that he learnt in church "Be alert, stand firm in the faith, be brave, be strong" (1 Corinthians 16:13). Archangel Michael appeared to him again to heal his wounds. When the other prisoners saw this miracle they believed in Jesus and stopped worshipping the statues at once. That day, the evil Governor killed them for believing in Jesus and they all went to heaven to be with God forever.

The next day Lucianus and Abanoub travelled by ship to a city called Atrib. During their journey the heartless Governor ordered for Abanoub to be tied upside down from the mast of the ship. The soldiers hurt and made fun of Abanoub while cheering and dancing. Abanoub's nose started bleeding but the Lord had mercy on him. He sent his Archangel once more to heal Abanoub and He paralyzed the soldiers so they were not able to move.

The soldiers were very afraid and didn't know what was happening to them, they desperately begged Abanoub saying "Please, pray to your God to heal us". Despite all the harm they did to Abanoub he followed the word of the Lord which said "love your enemies and pray for those who persecute you" (Matthew 5: 44). Abanoub told them that help will come when they reach Atrib where everyone can see God's power. The white sails caught heavy winds and brought the ship quickly to the city.

When they reached Atrib the soldiers were healed, they were able to move again, just like Abanoub said. They threw their weapons on the ground, raised their hands and gave thanks to the one true God. The evil Governor was filled with anger, he ordered that they all be captured and put to death but because they believed in Jesus the soldiers were united with God in heaven. Many people became believers because they witnessed the miracle from the shore, they too stopped worshipping the statues and followed Jesus.

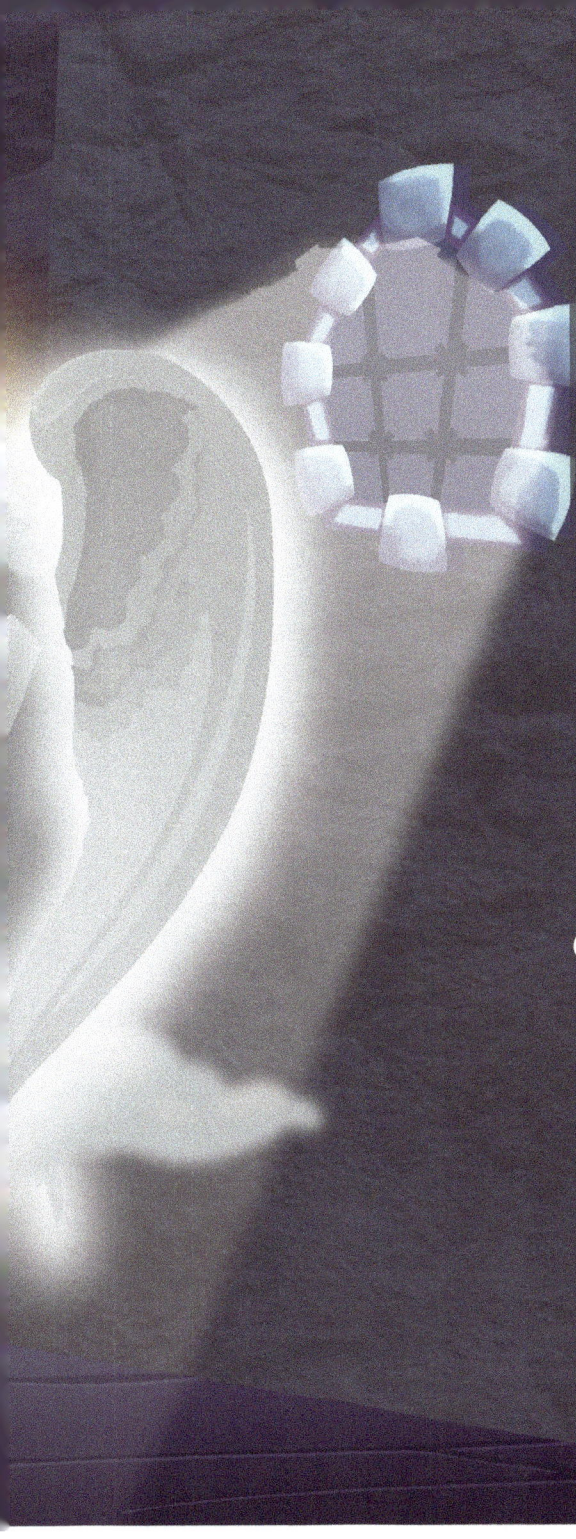

No matter what the Governor did, Abanoub prayed with the people in prison, smiling and praising the name of the Lord. There were many people who were amazed by how such a young boy could have so much strength, faith and courage while being in prison. News of Abanoub was spreading quickly, everyone who learnt about Jesus through Abanoub became Christian. This drove the Governor crazy, he continued to kill those who followed Jesus and looked for new ways to torture Abanoub.

God's power was revealed when He healed Abanoub, this made many people realise that the governor's statues were not true gods. Having no idea what to do next, Lucianus the evil Governor called some magicians to give him advice about how to win against Abanoub and his strong faith. They suggested locking the saint in a dungeon filled with poisonous snakes that would terrify even the strongest of people, the Governor agreed and ordered his guards to throw Abanoub in a dungeon filled with the most dangerous snakes in all the land.

Abanoub had no fear, he knew that if God managed to save Daniel the prophet from the lions, He could also save him from these poisonous snakes. The next morning when they opened the dungeon they were sure he was not going to be alive, to their surprise they found Abanoub happy in prayer, unharmed by the snakes. When the magicians saw that the Lord protected Abanoub their hearts were transformed, they were sorry and believed in the Lord Jesus.

After three days of torturing Abanoub, Lucianus realised that the boy's faith was unshakable. He knew he could not overpower Abanoub's God so ordered his soldiers to kill Abanoub. Abanoub became a martyr who would spend eternity with Jesus in heaven. A Christian named Julius wrapped Abanoub's body and took it back to his hometown of Nehisa. Years later his remains were moved to the church in Samanoud. Saint Abanoub performed many miracles and continues to perform miracles even until this day.

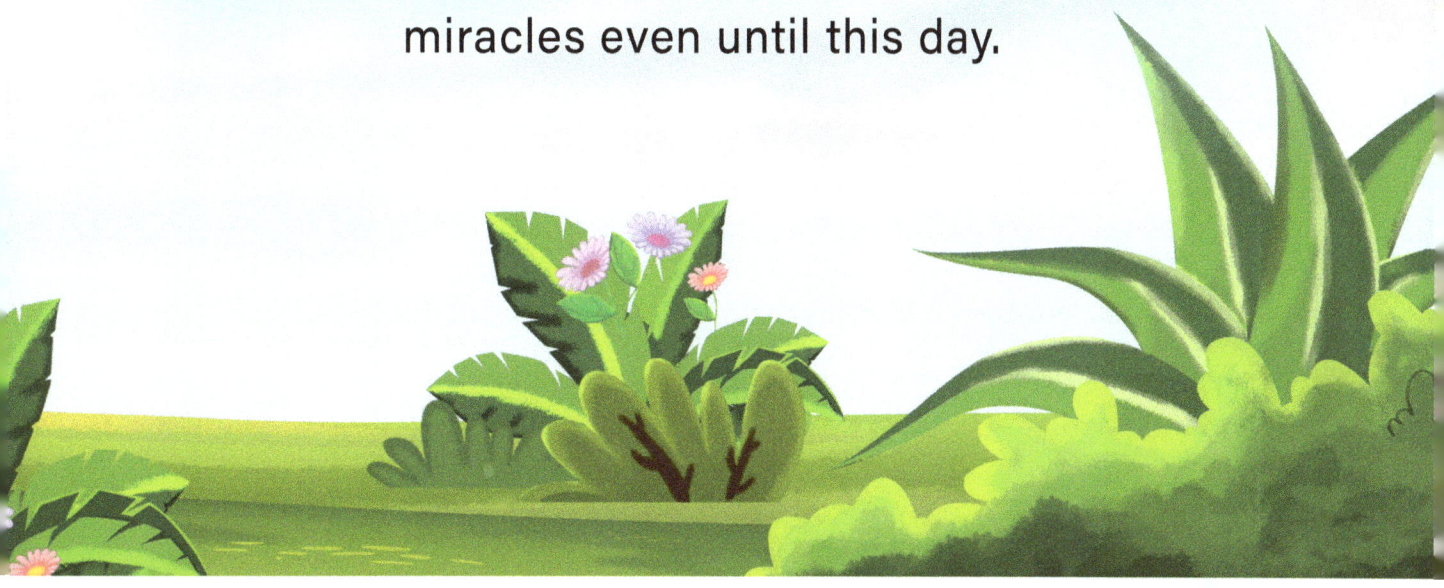

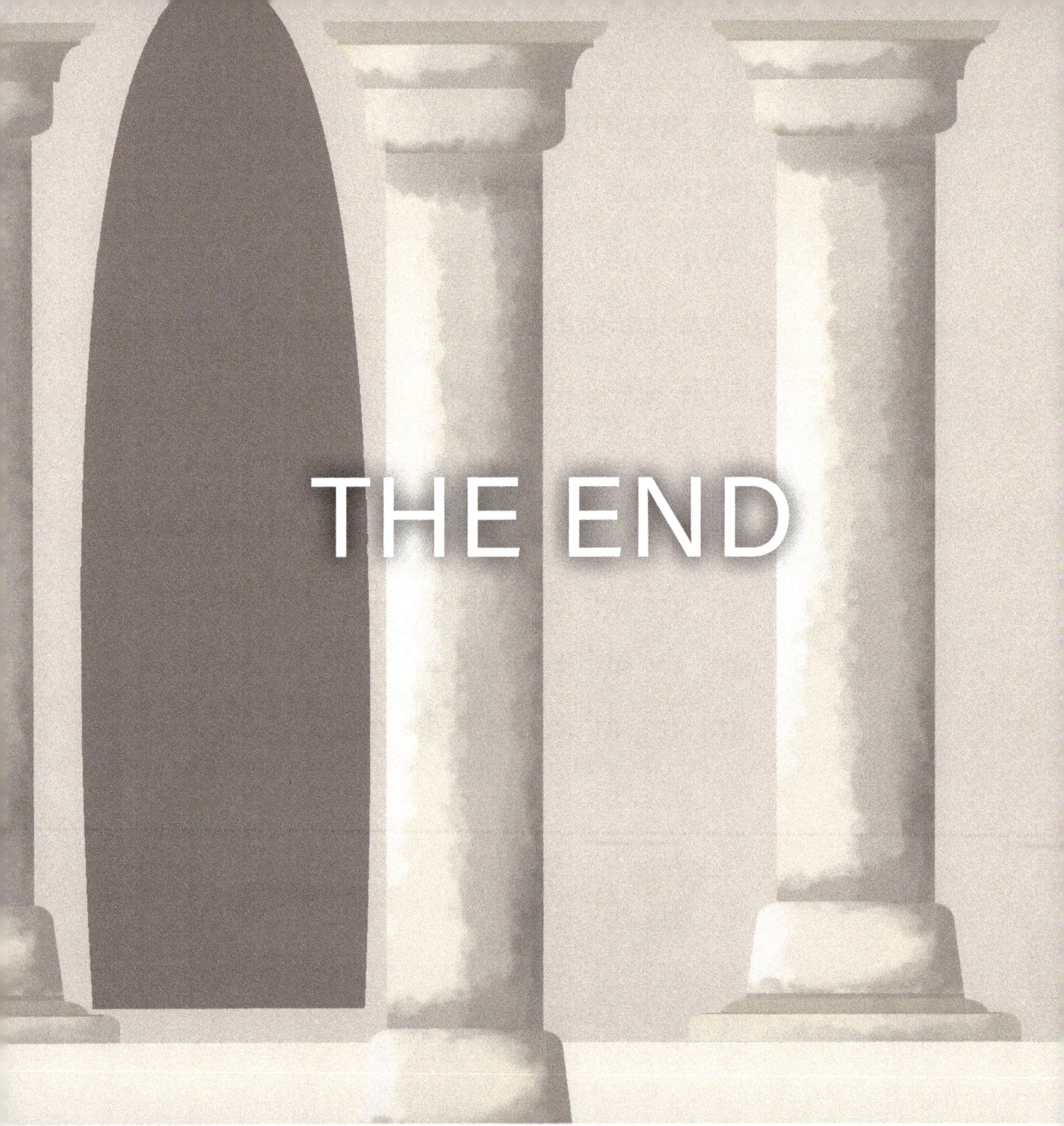
THE END

www.ingramcontent.com/pod-product-compliance
Lightning Source LLC
Chambersburg PA
CBHW060856090426
42736CB00024B/3493